*Priests*

# Priests

## An Inside Look

Rev. John P. Mack Jr.

Saint Mary's Press
Christian Brothers Publications
Winona, Minnesota

Genuine recycled paper with 10% post-consumer waste.
Printed with soy-based ink.

The publishing team included Shirley Kelter, development editor; Paul Grass, FSC, copy editor; Brooke Saron, production editor; Hollace Storkel, typesetter; Laurie Geisler, art director; cover and inside image by W. P. Wittman Limited; manufactured by the production services department of Saint Mary's Press.

The acknowledgments continue on page 65.

Printed in the United States of America

Printing: 9 8 7 6 5 4 3 2 1

Year: 2009 08 07 06 05 04 03 02 01

ISBN 0-88489-720-6

Library of Congress Cataloging-in-Publication Data

Mack, John P., 1954–
      Priests: an inside look / John P. Mack Jr.
      p. cm.
      Includes bibliographical references.
ISBN 0-88489-720-6 (pbk.)
      1. Priesthood—Catholic Church. 2. Vocation, Ecclesiastical. [1. Priesthood—Catholic Church. 2. Catholic Church—Clergy. 3. Vocation, Ecclesiastical.] I. Title.
BX1912 .M19 2002
262'.142—dc21

                                                                    2001001797

*To my parents, John and Lucille Mack,*
*who first formed me in faith*

# Contents

# Series Foreword

An old Hasidic legend about the mysterious nature of life says that God whispers into your newly created soul all the secrets of your existence, all the divine love for you, and your unique purpose in life. Then, just as God infuses your soul into your body, an assisting angel presses your mouth shut and instructs your soul to forget its preternatural life.

You are now spending your time on earth seeking to know once again the God who created you, loves you, and assigns you a singular purpose. Raise your forefinger to feel the crease mark the angel left above your lips, and ask yourself in wonder: Who am I? How am I uniquely called to live in the world?

The authors of the five titles in this Vocations series tell how they approached these same questions as they searched for meaning and purpose in their Christian vocation, whether as a brother, a married couple, a priest, a single person, or a sister.

Christians believe that God creates a dream for each person. What is your dream in life? This is how Pope John Paul II, echoing Jeremiah 1:5, speaks of the Creator's dream and the divine origin of your vocation:

All human beings, from their mothers' womb, belong to God who searches them and knows them, who forms them and knits them together with his own hands, who gazes on them when they are tiny shapeless embryos and already sees in them the adults of tomorrow whose days are numbered and whose vocation is even now written in the "book of life." (*Evangelium Vitae,* no. 61)

In spite of believing that God does have your specific vocation in mind, you probably share the common human experience—the tension and the mystery—of finding out who you are and how God is personally calling you to live in this world. Although you can quickly recognize the uniqueness of your thumbprint, you will spend a lifetime deciphering the full meaning of your originality.

There is no shortage of psychological questionnaires for identifying your personality type, career path, learning style, and even a compatible mate. Although these methods can be helpful in your journey to self-discovery, they do little to illuminate the mystery in your quest. What is the best approach to knowing your vocation in life? Follow the pathway as it unfolds before you, and live with the questions that arise along the way.

The stories in this Vocations series tell about life on the path of discernment and choice; they remind you that you are not alone. God is your most present and patient companion. In the "travelogues" of these authors, you will find reassurance that even when you relegate the Divine Guide to keeping ten paces behind you or when you abandon the path entirely for a time, you cannot undo God's faithfulness to you. Each vocation story uniquely testifies to the truth that God is always at work revealing your life's purpose to you.

In these stories you will also find that other traveling companions—family, friends, and classmates—contribute to your discovery of a place in the world and call forth the person you are becoming. Their companionship along the way not only manifests God's abiding presence but also reminds you to respect others for their gifts, which highlight and mirror your own.

Although each path in the Vocations series is as unique as the person who tells his or her story, these accounts remind you to be patient with the mystery of your own life, to have confidence in God's direction, and to listen to the people and events you encounter as you journey to discover your unique role in God's plan. By following your path, you too will come to see the person of tomorrow who lives in you today.

Clare vanBrandwijk

# A Genesis

We declare to you what was from the beginning, what we have heard, what we have seen with our eyes, what we have looked at and touched with our hands, concerning the word of life—this life was revealed, and we have seen it and testify to it, and declare to you the eternal life that was with the Father and was revealed to us—we declare to you what we have seen and heard so that you also may have fellowship with us; and truly our fellowship is with the Father and with his Son Jesus Christ. We are writing these things so that our joy may be complete. (1 John 1:1–4)

*I think I might have a vocation.* That remains one of the hardest statements I have ever made. I uttered these words over twenty years ago to a priest assigned to the parish where I worshiped. That priest simply said in reply: "You might. Let's talk about it." My journey started with that conversation and continued through four years in the seminary, three pastoral assignments, and countless Sunday homilies and eucharistic celebrations. Now this vocation journey includes writing my thoughts in this book. The path has encompassed unexpected twists and turns, many accomplishments matched by as many mistakes, and a mixture of joy, sadness, growth, and regret.

I am twenty years into preparing for and serving as an ordained Roman Catholic priest (including seminary formation), and my vocation still strikes me as unbelievable and overwhelming! I pinch myself daily in disbelief that the Catholic church, with the help of God, entrusts me with servant leadership through priestly ordination.

*No one right story or unique way*
*to embark on the journey exists*
*except to remain true to the person*
*God calls you to be.*

The genesis of my out-of-this-world journey is hidden deep within the recesses of my forty-six-year story, a narrative emerging from the life stories of my parents, grandparents, family members (from Catholic and other faith traditions), and friends. No one right story or unique way to embark on the journey exists except to remain true to the person God calls you to be.

There are as many paths on the journey to priesthood as there are priests. My parents' post–World War II wedding was a "mixed" marriage (between a Catholic and a baptized Protestant). My father did not convert to Roman Catholicism until a few years into the marriage. Because the wedding occurred before Vatican Council II, the ceremony took place in the rectory, not in the church building, because my father wasn't Catholic. My mother and her family attended Mass and received Communion in church before going over to the rectory for the wedding. I am certain that the possibility of having an ordained priest from that marriage bond seemed remote at the time.

The first step on my priestly journey could have been the result of an offhand word of encouragement spoken decades ago by one of my godparents. Maybe the vocation seed was planted in wonderful childhood memories wrapped in the mysterious patina of a dark, candlelit church or in the glancing light reflected from a gold chalice elevated by a priest before the worshiping congregation.

The priests of my childhood memories are not distinct. Rather, they seem otherworldly, distant, and powerful, dressed in ornate clothing while performing familiar ritual actions Sunday after Sunday. To this child, church appeared bigger than life. For all the young at heart, I hope this remains the case well into adulthood.

The true divine beginnings of a priestly vocation precede all these possible explanations, as Pope John Paul II writes:

All human beings, from their mothers' womb, belong to God who searches them and knows them, who forms them and knits them together with his own hands, who gazes on them when they are tiny shapeless embryos and already sees in them the adults of tomorrow whose days are numbered and whose vocation is even now written in the "book of life." (*Evangelium Vitae,* no. 61)

Writing about the priesthood vocation gives me pause to reflect on my own vocation in the God-given favor of ordained priesthood. My voice and the voices of the other priests in this book speak in heartfelt hope that our stories may stir into faith and action the heart of readers who may be searching for their own calling. Our stories are unique, but they provide a glimpse of the great variety that is Roman Catholic priesthood and the diversity that is the church itself.

I have attempted to paint a contemporary portrait of ordained ministry by following the structure and content of the traditional ordination ritual: from the call through the laying on of hands, from the words of consecration to the first blessing imparted by the newly ordained priest. This picture is limited to the palette of colors I have available, including the diocese I serve (Buffalo, New York), the seminary I attended (Christ the King Seminary, East Aurora, New York), and the assorted priests I have encountered during my fifteen-plus years of ordained service.

I have asked a variety of folks, including young people, what a reader might find interesting about the priesthood. Their suggested topics served as a springboard for my writing. I have attempted to address a wide-ranging audience: from the young man who is seriously consider-ing ordained ministry to the curious bystander who casually picks up this volume.

*This work is intended . . . to serve as a gateway for questioning and for greater involvement in the life of the church.*

This work is intended not to be exhaustive but rather to serve as a gateway for questioning and for greater involvement in the life of the church. Writing about priesthood vocations, including my own, and fol-lowing the words of the *Rite of Ordination of a Priest* as a guide have prompted considerable self-reflection. Reflecting anew on the bishop's homiletic instruction, the ordination prayer of consecration, the ques-tions, and the promise of obedience has been rewarding and renewing for me in my ordained ministry. The passage of time clouds over the clar-ity of all these words and the feelings that accompany them; yet, I see the results in my day-to-day ministry.

Words that I do vividly recall from ordination are those of my bishop, the Most Reverend Edward D. Head, now the retired bishop of Buffalo. He used to say in his remarks at ordination that priesthood "is the great-est fraternity in the world." I continue to discover the meaning of his words; in that spirit I present this reflection for consideration by all who wonder.

# The Call to Priesthood

## Scratching the Surface

The ordained ministerial priesthood remains one of the few life vocations still referred to as a "calling." I am not sure that most people consider sacramental marriage to be a calling, although it is certainly a sacramental life vocation in the church for the world and a symbol of Christ's love for the church.

People used to think that teaching in the classroom or working in the medical arts presumed a vocational calling, perhaps because the nature of the teacher's, doctor's, and nurse's work requires the extra strength of divine intervention! Education and medicine were envisioned as fields that attract individuals primarily interested in helping other people through a humanitarian desire rooted in an otherworldly calling. A feeling in the heart almost obligated people to move into these fields.

I used to think that the calling would sound from the heavens in an audible voice, perhaps deep and booming like the voice heard in biblical epics on the silver screen. With such a voice calling, I would know for sure if it were meant for me. There could be no mistake about it. I could hear the calling and respond, "Yes, Lord, I read you loud and clear. 10–4. Roger, over and out."

*The calling is much subtler,*
*like an itch that longs to be scratched.*

The calling to ordained ministry is not that clear. I did not wake up one day, hear a voice, and immediately pick up the phone to dial the seminary. The calling is much subtler, like an itch that longs to be scratched. Examining the surface of the skin doesn't immediately reveal what is causing you to want to scratch. But something is there below the surface, seeking your attention and a response—one way or another.

Now I certainly do not equate God's calling you to the priesthood vocation with an irritating itch that just will not go away! However, it can happen that there is a Divine Patience and Persistence gently massaging your heart, preparing you to consider a life of servant leadership in the church. Before you know it, you begin thinking about a role—a role of service and of leadership, an ordained role that you might never have considered likely or possible.

My story is probably not much different than anyone else's. I was not knocked off my horse, as Saint Paul experienced on the road to Damascus. As I was riding my high horse into adult life, my calling to the priesthood began more like a saddle sore than a knockdown bolt of lightning. In fact, my early twenty-something years contained not so much a calling as an *inkling* that I wanted to help people. I just was not sure where or how I would do this.

I attended Kent State University in the early 1970s, a tumultuous time on that campus, following the shooting deaths of four students during anti–Vietnam war demonstrations. The political climate on that campus strengthened in me an understanding of what it means to be committed to a cause. In the four years I was there, the faculty and student body struggled with the truth of why these young people were gunned down by Ohio National Guard troops. Then, it affected me—I'd never been exposed to that degree of commitment—and today, I understand that the seeds of justice and peace were planted in me, later to be lived out in my vocation.

I graduated at the age of twenty-one from Kent State University, in June 1975. With a bachelor's degree in communications in hand, I knew what I had wanted to do since I was an awkward teenager at Monroe High School in Rochester, New York: work in broadcasting, radio in particular. Get ready, world, here I come!

Obviously, the world was not ready. The dozens of résumés I sent out during my waning days of college landed me only one job interview. Miraculously, that audition led to a job offer at a small-town radio station in the picturesque Finger Lakes region of upstate New York. Boy, I thought I was pretty important, a big fish in a small town, with live on-air work, including news and early talk-radio programs: people would call in and promote their garage sales — every day! I composed news stories (mostly rewritten from the local daily newspaper), wrote and recorded commercials, did live remotes, and even provided color commentary for the broadcasts of high school football and basketball games. I thought, "This is the life!" I was doing what I knew I wanted to do, and I was closely connected to a community through the medium of radio.

My job was my whole life. I had little time for or interest in relationships, and I gave less thought to my faith life. In college I enjoyed the guitar Masses in the Newman Center at Kent State University. They were true celebrations of faith geared to an age group of young people searching for their way. These liturgies reflected the changing times of the 1970s. After graduating from the college scene and now living on my own, I attended the local parish church on occasion. The Masses were not the same, but religion and spirituality as a whole were on the periphery of my thought.

Sure, I was Roman Catholic, I told myself. This was as much a part of my identity as my ethnic heritage. My parents and I went to church regularly as I grew up, but I did not attend Catholic schools (too expensive, my factory-worker father thought), and I became what was popularly referred to as one of the "publics": Catholics considered to be not as committed as those who attended Catholic schools. This unfortunate stigma from the past remains to this day.

Yet, as I look back now, I see the Divine Hand at work through the diverse helping hands that guided me during those times, including the hard-working, loving hands of my parents, who first helped me stand on my own two feet. Those guiding hands also include the mentoring of the general manager and the receptionist at that first radio station job, who helped me to mature. Gently guiding me as well were the local, truly wise, and hard-working print journalists, the actors and singers from the community theater group that I joined to do mid-1970s productions of Gilbert and Sullivan operettas, and the landlords who rented me apartments and didn't rip me off despite my post-college naïveté. The church was always there in the background, tucked away in a dusty corner of my mind. The sacramental presence of Christ in the church silently and patiently watched throughout my youthful wanderings and waited for me to find myself in those first years after college.

When I moved from one western New York community to another because of a job transfer in 1977, ordination and priesthood were probably the farthest things from my mind. That was the year the King of Rock and Roll, Elvis Presley, died. I was more interested in Top 40 music formats than in sacraments and matters of the spirit.

Yet, Christ, the Sovereign of the Universe, continued cultivating that inkling within me, leading me step by step to greater active participation in the life of the church. A parish priest saw that glimmer in me before I could even imagine such a thing myself. He helped me discover that divinely implanted inkling.

*Quickly, without a conscious effort,*
*I was drawn into the pastoral, ministerial,*
*and liturgical life of the church.*

With this priest's encouragement, I began to serve as a lector at Sunday Mass. Maybe I was asked to do that because I had a good radio announcer's voice. The Scriptures themselves remained a great mystery yet to unfold within my life. Before becoming a lector, I ran errands at the parish's spring festival. Soon, I received diocesan training to serve as a special minister of Holy Communion. I helped write the prayers of the faithful for Sunday Mass. Eventually, I was present for more than one Mass each weekend. Quickly, without a conscious effort, I was drawn into the pastoral, ministerial, and liturgical life of the church.

I wanted to do these church activities, assist at liturgies, and become involved in a leadership role in the life of the church. Only after four years of priestly formation at the seminary, four years of graduate-level classes leading to a master of divinity degree, and my first couple of ministerial assignments would I begin to understand what ordained ministry is all about.

Each person's call to ordained ministry is unique. A friend from the Diocese of Rochester, Fr. Michael Bausch, shares this story:

> I did not seriously begin to think about the priesthood until I was out of college three years and began to realize the church was bigger than going to Mass. I was involved in the recovery efforts from a major natural disaster in 1973 (Hurricane Agnes and the resulting floods in the southern tier of New York State), and as a result of my contact with Catholic relief organizations, I came to realize that the church could help people in the midst of a very real crisis. For me the church took on a human face and was more than the sacredness of the church building. Consequently, priesthood became a real possibility for my future and me.

Another friend, Fr. Dan Palys, from the Diocese of Buffalo, recalls:

> When I was fourteen, I loved to go to Mass because I was an altar server. I began serving right after making my first Holy Communion in second grade. I served Mass every day for over twelve years. I never missed daily Mass. I loved the priests—I was inspired by them.
>
> I am one of those rare people who wanted to be a priest from the earliest age. I cannot remember a time I did not want to be a priest.

## The Call

*"Let those who are to be ordained priest please come forward."* This simple sentence, spoken by a deacon at the beginning of the Rite of Ordination, constitutes "the call" that comes from God and is expressed through the voice of the church. Each candidate, when called by name, answers, "Present," and makes a sign of reverence (a bow) to the ordaining bishop, who presides at the ceremony. Then a priest, such as the vocation director or the director of seminarians, says to the bishop, "Most Reverend Father, holy mother Church asks you to ordain these men, our brothers, for service as priest."

The ordaining bishop asks, "Do you judge them to be worthy?" The designated spokesman replies, "After inquiry among the people of Christ and upon recommendation of those concerned with their training, I testify that they have been found worthy." Then the bishop declares, "We rely on the help of the Lord God and our Savior Jesus Christ, and we choose these men, our brothers, for priesthood in the presbyteral order."

Usually, thunderous applause follows, and heartfelt accolades from family, friends, parishioners, and fellow ordained ministers cascade in waves over each candidate, who stands humbled by the loving support of the faithful gathered for this solemn ceremony.

*Ordination is a public celebration of a deeply personal process that unfolds within the human heart.*

The Rite of Ordination publicly proclaims a soul-searching discernment and formation process that takes years for each candidate. Ordination is a public celebration of a deeply personal process that unfolds within the human heart. Many different roads lead each priesthood ordination candidate to respond wholeheartedly to the call with the word, *Present*.

At 7 p.m. on Saturday, 1 June 1985 (feast of the Holy Trinity), at a large parish church in suburban Buffalo, New York, I responded to the call from the diocesan leader, Bishop Edward D. Head. Literally and figuratively, at 6 feet 6 inches tall, he stood head and shoulders above me. I was thirty-one years of age, the second oldest in the group of eight men who were ordained that year to the priesthood for the diocese of Buffalo.

Each of us chose to be ordained in a parish church, either his home parish or the one he had served as a transitional deacon in the preceding year. Ordinations usually take place at the cathedral, the main church of the diocese, where the bishop presides from the *cathedra*, his seat of authority. We had been ordained to the order of deacon at Saint Joseph's Cathedral the year before, on 11 May 1984, one day after our graduation from Christ the King Seminary in East Aurora, New York, an idyllic country setting half an hour from downtown Buffalo.

## *A chorus of human voices expresses the Divine Call within the church.*

The four years of priesthood formation, prayerful discernment, and graduate studies lead to the formal call to priesthood. With the help of God, that formation process enables the candidate to respond, "Present," to the call at his ordination ceremony. The priestly ministry for each candidate flows from this ceremony.

Through fifteen years of experience, I now look back at that ordination day and am reminded of the call, of my response, "Present," and of the applause and the sea of loving support as I sink or swim, years later, in the day-to-day reality of ministry. A chorus of human voices expresses the Divine Call within the church in all their consoling, challenging, irritating, and questioning tones: gray-haired grandmothers, squirming children, mitered bishops, pastors old and young, deacons permanent and transitional. In turn, the call empowers me to give voice, to respond, "Present," and to be present to a sacramental people of Christ by means of a sacramental presence from Holy Orders.

As is the case with any "Present," priesthood is truly a gift. The call, the response, the service, the joys, the challenges, the opportunities, the growth—even the doubts—are all part of the gift that is priesthood, one that is unwrapped, treasured, utilized, and shared, all in due time. The gift to be present and to lead within the church as an ordained priest first resides as an invitation quietly placed in the heart and nudged forward through an inkling of a desire to serve others. The gift never comes too early, too late, or delayed (as people used to call those who enter the seminary several years after college graduation). The gift comes "all in good time"—God's time. This gift, as with any gift, is most appreciated when the recipient passes it around, like the favorite family casserole at a potluck supper, the photographs of a special celebration, or the stories about activities of great importance. The gift, never solely for the recipient's benefit, is uniquely bestowed so that he can answer his unique call to priesthood with "Present!"

# The Roots of Priesthood and Formation Today

## For Ever in No Time at All

> Christ the Lord, a priest for ever in the line of Melchizedek, offered bread and wine. (*Rite of Ordination of a Priest*, no. 25)

*"Tu es sacerdos in aeternum"*—a beautiful, handmade, three-color calligraphy of the Latin verse from Psalm 110:4 ("You are a priest forever")—hangs in a gold metallic frame on my bedroom wall. This ordination gift from a parishioner I met during my year as a transitional deacon serves as a daily reminder of the eternal mystery that I entered at ordination and of the timelessness of day-to-day ministry.

Marriage is until "death do you part"; priesthood is "for ever," which seems like a very long time. In truth, eternity is no time at all!

If you reflect on the eternal nature of priesthood, you will discover that the word *priesthood*, as handed down in Catholic Tradition and rooted in the Scriptures, contains multiple meanings for the Christian life. An understanding of *sacrifice* and *religion* is helpful in comprehending priesthood and the notion of "for ever."

The bishop's instruction during the ordination ceremony reminds the assembled community:

It is true that God has made his entire people a royal priesthood in Christ. But our High Priest, Jesus Christ, also chose some of his followers to carry out publicly in the Church a priestly ministry in his name on behalf of mankind. He was sent by the Father, and he in turn sent the apostles into the world; through them and their successors, the bishops, he continues his work as Teacher, Priest, and Shepherd. Priests are co-workers of the order of bishops. They are joined to the bishops in the priestly office and are called to serve God's people. (*Rite of Ordination of a Priest,* no. 13)

At their baptism into Christ and their baptismal anointing in Christ as priest, prophet, and king, Christians are formed into "a royal priesthood." As the First Letter of Peter says:

But you are a chosen race, a royal priesthood, a holy nation, God's own people, in order that you may proclaim the mighty acts of him who called you out of darkness into his marvelous light. (2:9)

These New Testament words echo the Old Testament, when God makes a Covenant with Israel through Moses:

You shall be for me a priestly kingdom and a holy nation. These are the words that you shall speak to the Israelites. (Exodus 19:6)

The entire faith community is portrayed as priestly in nature. This priestly identity intimately connects them to the ordained priesthood as first descended from Aaron, the brother of Moses. The ordained priest acts on behalf of the priestly people as a whole.

The ordained priest serves as the bearer of sacrifice. In ancient times, sacrifice included animal and harvest offerings to God. Christians center on the Sacrifice of Christ, the High Priest (especially as described in Saint Paul's Letter to the Hebrews), and ordained priests now preside at the offering of the Sacrifice of the Mass. *Sacrifice* is one of those words freely tossed about that has changed in meaning over time. Because the ordained priest is concerned with the work of sacrifice, it is a good idea to investigate the roots of the word to discover what sacrifice is and why Christians perform it as part of their religion.

According to *Merriam-Webster,* the word *sacrifice* comes from the Latin word *sacrificium,* "to make sacred." Although the popular meaning of sacrifice is "to give up something," people of faith believe that the essential action of sacrifice is "to make sacred."

*We become what we receive,*
> *Christ's Body and Blood,*
*so that we in turn can be*
> *bread and wine . . . for other people.*

What is made sacred by the action of a sacrifice? Although Christians do not offer animal sacrifices and grain offerings, in the sacrament of the Eucharist, they bring to the altar of sacrifice the simple gifts of bread and wine, offered in thanks and praise. Jesus Christ identifies himself with bread and wine, as you learn in the Gospel description of the Last Supper. Bread and wine become Christ's Body and Blood, which you and I receive at Communion so that we can be sacred as a priestly people. We become what we receive, Christ's Body and Blood, so that we in turn can be bread and wine, food and drink, for other people in their spiritual quest to make sacred their own life. The priestly people receive the liturgical sacrifice of thanks and praise (the Eucharist) as thanksgiving (the Greek word *eucharist* means "gratitude"). As a body, the Christian people receive what it offers, and more!

Christians then go forth, as a priestly people and a holy nation, to announce with gratitude God's praises to the ends of the earth—which are not really all that far away, for they remain as close as the spiritual journey that the human heart embarks on.

Christians cannot separate the sacred realm of sacrifice from the secular world of day-to-day living. In fact, it was amid secular society that I experienced my call to ordained ministry. Pulling up the drawbridge and withdrawing in fearful condemnation of the world are not Christian options.

Office, grocery store, school, mall, coffee shop, and factory are the places you are "to make sacred" through your Gospel life. Relationships with coworkers, children, parents, spouse, neighbors, and strangers are where you live Christ's great commandment to love God, neighbor, and self. Church cannot remain trapped within four walls.

> *Office, grocery store, school, mall, coffee shop, and factory are the places you are "to make sacred" through your Gospel life.*

Together as a priestly people, you and I continue to make sacred our world. This "together" aspect speaks to what we Christians are about in religion, another word used without much awareness of its original meaning. *Religion* comes from the Latin *religare,* "to restrain, tie back," and from *ligatus,* "ligaments" connected in a bond (ligature). Restraint, at first hearing, seems to have a negative meaning. However, think of ligaments that restrain and tie the bones together and support the internal organs. Ligaments are the key to unlocking an understanding of religion in relation to bonds.

For example, bonds of meaning emerge from the bonds of religion. Bonds of connection between the divine and the human, as well as among people, find expression within religious practice. Sacrifice ritualizes bonds of shared purpose. Bonds make Christians a faith community led by its servant leader, the ordained priest.

27

Priests

The ordained priest's own purpose is linked in an unbreakable bond with the meaning of sacrifice and the role of religion in the truest sense. The primary purpose of the priest, as a servant leader connected in ministry to a particular group of people, is to make sacred that group, empowering a holy people in bonds of belief, charity, and hope. The priest actively performs this role through the sacramental life of the church, in which he participates through the sacrament of Holy Orders.

The priest is concerned about the things of forever: eternity, time-lessness, God. He also focuses on the things of the here and now: cre-ation, mortality, timeliness, humanity. The priest stands with clay feet firmly planted on the earth in hopes of the celestial haven of the Creator and grounded in the present reality of the human domain of creation. Delicate movement through both of these realms marks the priest's faith journey as he walks with care through God's earthly garden toward the Reign of God.

## Priesthood Patterns: Stripes and Plaids

"Father, what kind of priest are you anyway: a Jesuit, Franciscan, or something?" I always wonder what people mean by the "or something" comment. Depending on the questioner's sense of humor, sometimes I respond by saying, "Oh, I am just a normal priest." My Franciscan and Jesuit friends might take offense at my definition of "normal" priest. After all, a priest is a priest is a priest.

Despite my lame attempt at humor, how and where the ministerial priest lives his ordained life does differ, like stripes and plaids. These vari-ations in priesthood patterns stem from how and where the church calls the priest to serve. The call comes either through the *charism* (a gift of the Spirit) of a particular religious order or from a diocese.

Priests ordained for service to a diocese are known as secular priests (from the Latin *saeculum,* meaning "world"). They serve their ministry within the world as diocesan clergy. Secular, or diocesan, priests do not live within a religious community, although they may live in small groups within a parish rectory. Diocesan priests minister within a specific diocese and cannot easily move from place to place. In fact, all ordained priests have to belong to a specific entity, such as a diocese or a religious congregation (or be "incardinated," in the case of a diocesan priest who transfers to a diocese other than the one in which he was ordained). No "free agents" are allowed, as in professional sports or in Christian denominations that have a congregational form of organization and governance.

## The spirituality of the diocesan priest is rooted in the life of the parish community.

The call to ministry within the Roman Catholic church is by diocese or religious community, not by individual parish. My ministerial identity as a diocesan priest comes from my life lived within the parish and the diocese I serve. The spirituality of the diocesan priest is rooted in the life of the parish community and in ministry to its members.

"Religious" priests are ordained to serve within a religious order or congregation, such as Franciscans, Dominicans, Benedictines, and Jesuits. They minister, pray, and live in the light of a religious identity inspired by the charism of the order's founder (such as Saint Francis) or the Rule (such as the one written by Saint Benedict). Religious priests are consecrated in ordination (the sacrament of Orders) and through their profession of religious vows. They have a dual identity: ordained minister and member of a religious community. The religious priest lives his priesthood vocation within the religious congregation to which he belongs. He may serve within a parish or another institution, such as a school or a hospital. Unlike the diocesan priest, the religious priest develops his identity from the charism of the religious order and finds his community with the members of that order.

Roman Catholic priests make ordination promises to obey their Ordinary (the bishop and his successors) or their religious superior and to live a celibate life. Vows are not part of the ordination ritual itself. Religious priests make vows of poverty, chastity, and obedience at the time of their profession in their religious community. Women religious (nuns and sisters) and men religious (brothers) make similar vows as consecrated laity in a community. Men religious who are preparing for the priesthood profess their vows prior to ordination.

*I developed my understanding and appreciation of the power of ritual to transform hearts and lives.*

## Planting of Seeds

My years spent in priestly formation and graduate studies at Christ the King Seminary during the early 1980s still rank as four of the happiest years of my life. I thrived in the heady atmosphere of theological and scriptural studies, prayer, and camaraderie. Well-prepared liturgies and music served to develop my faith and stood as a central component of my priestly formation. In the sacred space and time that enveloped the seminary, I developed my understanding and appreciation of the power of ritual to transform hearts and lives.

According to the revised *Code of Canon Law,* candidates for the priesthood must have completed five years of philosophical and theo-logical studies before ordination to the diaconate (canon 1032). After the candidate has earned a baccalaureate degree, he completes a period of philosophical and theological study at a major seminary. The length of the transitional diaconate before priesthood ordination varies from diocese to diocese, although canonically it must be at least six months. Candidates for priesthood must have reached the age of twenty-five (canon 1031 allows the conference of bishops to increase the minimum age), possess maturity, and be confirmed in the Catholic church. Before ordination the priesthood candidate must experience a five-day retreat.

Formation for religious-order priests is somewhat different and can vary from order to order. Fr. Jim Vacco, a Franciscan, offers this reflection on formation:

> For priests of religious orders, there is a tension between the call to religious community and the call to priesthood. The first part of Franciscan formation is common for all candidates who enter religious life—whether they intend to become priests or brothers. There is at least a year of "affiliation," a transition to community life. Affiliates take classes about religious life and do apostolic ministry in the field. Following the affiliate time there is a sixteen-month "novitiate" that is a more intense preparation time, regimented with study, prayer, and spiritual direction. At the end of the novitiate, temporary four-year vows are taken. During those four years, priest-candidates study theology while brothers in the community study a year of theology plus a profession such as teaching or counseling (this will vary according to the charism and mission of the religious order). At the end of the four years, final vows are professed.

Seminary formation became the norm in the church following the Council of Trent (1545–1563). The bishops in council were attempting to re-establish the practice of priestly formation at a cathedral school, which had fallen into disuse during medieval times because of the rise of universities as centers of scholarly learning. The church had moved far away from its early history when bishops took personal responsibility for priestly formation.

By the beginning of the Protestant Reformation, early in the sixteenth century, the church was not adequately preparing priests theologically to face the rigors of ordained life. Restoration of diocesan seminaries for priestly formation would rectify that problem. By 1564, following the conclusion of the Council of Trent, seminaries were opening in Italy and

Germany, and the seventeenth century saw seminaries flourishing in France. But problems in the late eighteenth century resulted in the closing of some seminaries in Western Europe.

The political independence of the United States, late in the eighteenth century, created the need for seminary formation on the other side of the Atlantic Ocean. Although the Council of Trent had called for a seminary in every diocese, the United States bishops founded regional seminaries, beginning with Saint Mary's Seminary in Baltimore in 1791. The Councils of Baltimore (there were ten between 1829 and 1869) provided the basis for the development of the seminary system in the United States to this day. Although the first half of the twentieth century saw an explosion of growth in the number of seminaries and seminarians, the numbers have been in steady decline since the 1960s.

Despite this trend, the mandate for seminary formation remains clear: "The church has the duty and the proper and exclusive right to form those who are commissioned for the sacred ministries" (canon 232).

Young men who intend to enter the priesthood are to be given a suitable spiritual formation and trained for the duties of the priesthood in a major seminary throughout the entire time of formation, or, if circumstances demand it in the judgment of the diocesan bishop, at least for four years. (Canon 235)

The *Code of Canon Law* also specifies the criteria for admission to the seminary:

The diocesan bishop is to admit to the major seminary only those who are judged capable of dedicating themselves permanently to the sacred ministries in light of their human, moral, spiritual, and intellectual characteristics, their physical and psychological health, and their proper motivation. (Canon 241)

Canon law also defines the type of formation program to be offered to future priests:

The spiritual formation of the students in the seminary and their doctrinal instruction are to be harmonized and arranged so that in accord with the unique character of each student, they acquire the spirit of the Gospel and a close relationship with Christ along with appropriate human maturity. (Canon 244)

Through their spiritual formation, the students are to become equipped to exercise fruitfully the pastoral ministry, and they are to be formed in a missionary spirit; in the course of their formation, they are to learn that a ministry which is always carried out in living faith and in charity fosters their own sanctity; they are to learn to cultivate those virtues which are highly valued in human relations so that they can achieve an appropriate integration of human and supernatural qualities. (Canon 245)

Amen, I say, to all these directives!

## Pass It On

Meditate on the law of God, believe what you read, teach what you believe, and put into practice what you teach. (Bishop's homily, *Rite of Ordination of a Priest*, no. 14)

Meditate. Believe. Teach. Practice. These four actions constitute a continuous circle of spiritual growth for the ordained priest. As tempting as it might be for the priest to stop, pitch a tent, and relax in one of these four activities, grace calls the priest to move on. He must move forward, continuing on to the next level and ultimately to God, the "All in All" to whom he hands over everything.

*Meditate. Believe.
Teach. Practice.*

These words of instruction from *Rite of Ordination of a Priest* sound familiar to the candidate because he also heard them spoken at his diaconate ordination when he received the Book of the Gospels. "Believe, teach, and practice" serve as basics for ordained ministry, which is rooted in meditation on the living word of God. Prayer and ministry move together, hand in hand, in a joyful dance centered on God's real presence in Christ.

On the road to ordination are two ministries to which priesthood candidates are called during their seminary formation: the ministry of reader and of acolyte. Along with the Rite of Admission to Candidacy for Ordination, these two ministries replace numerous "minor orders" that had served for centuries as preparatory steps for those on their way to priesthood. Because the laity had already begun participating in the liturgy in some of these same ministries, including reading and altar service, Pope Paul VI reformed and clarified matters in an apostolic letter in 1972. Entry into the clerical state would now occur at diaconate ordination and not before, and participation in the ministries of the word and the altar would be required before the ordination of deacons and priests.

Either a bishop or the major superior of a religious community performs the Institution of Readers; their responsibilities include the following:

- proclaiming the word (except the Gospel) at liturgy
- leading the Psalm response and presenting the general intercessions in the absence of the cantor or the deacon
- leading the singing and the participation by the faithful at Mass
- instructing children and adults who are preparing to receive the sacraments

The homiletic instruction during the Institution of Readers states:

In proclaiming God's word to others, accept it yourselves in obedience to the Holy Spirit. Meditate on it constantly, so that each day you will have a deeper love of the Scriptures, and in all you say and do show forth to the world our Savior, Jesus Christ. (*The Institution of Readers and Acolytes*, no. 4)

The bishop or the religious superior gives the Bible to each candidate, saying:

Take this book of holy Scripture and be faithful in handing on the word of God, so that it may grow strong in the hearts of his people. (*The Institution of Readers and Acolytes*, no. 7)

The ministry of acolyte is threefold in nature:

- assisting the priest and deacon in service at the altar
- distributing Communion to the faithful at Mass and to those unable to attend because of illness
- placing the Blessed Sacrament in exposition for public adoration

The bishop instructs the candidates during the ceremony:

You should seek to understand the deep spiritual meaning of what you do, so that you may offer yourselves daily to God as spiritual sacrifices acceptable to him through Jesus Christ.

In performing your ministry bear in mind that, as you share the one bread with your brothers and sisters, so you form one body with them. Show a sincere love for Christ's Mystical Body, God's holy people, and especially for the weak and the sick. (*The Institution of Readers and Acolytes*, no. 4)

To be honest, I do not have a clear memory of my ceremonies of institution of the ministries of reader and acolyte, except that I am sure that following the formal event, we had wonderful trays of cakes and cookies prepared by the seminary dining room staff. What remain vividly in memory are my ministerial activities throughout seminary formation and in response to the institution of the ministries of reader and acolyte.

## *A never-ending story.*

A seminary classmate and I used to teach adult education every Monday evening at a neighborhood parish on the east side of Buffalo to a roomful of eager believers in their "third age" (that is, senior citizens). We taught the Scriptures, styles of prayer, liturgy and liturgical reforms, church history, and the sacraments. These students were like sponges, eager to soak up knowledge, inquisitive, and dedicated to updating their faith. In retrospect, I recognize that these older students passed on to their teachers more about faith than we could ever impart to them in our weekly classes.

This adult-education activity, which we had inherited from two fourth-year seminarians, was in addition to our official field education experiences at various parish, school, and medical facilities in the area. A deaf school, a college campus ministry's Newman Center, a cancer hospital, a homeless drop-in center, a soup kitchen, numerous nursing homes, and countless parishes served as learning and formation sites for seminarians. In these places of ministry, where Christ is served in the people who are hungry, thirsty, poor, fearful, eager, hopeful, and despairing, the never-ending circle of spiritual growth for the ordained priest emerged. Meditate. Believe. Teach. Practice. A never-ending story.

# Chapter 3

# The Sacrament of Holy Orders

## What's the Matter?

The heart and soul of each sacrament—its core, its essence—are *matter* and *form*. Determining the sacramental matter and form answers the question, "What is necessary for this sacrament to take place?" I leave the general discussion to the sacramental theologians who ponder such lofty questions. For my purposes, I want to examine what is at the heart of ordination and how the understanding of Holy Orders evolved during the church reforms of the twentieth century. This portrait of the past helps paint a picture of the present.

Reform of the liturgy began late in 1963, when newly elected Pope Paul VI promulgated the first of many dramatic changes produced by the Second Vatican Council, *Sacrosanctum Concilium* (the first two words of the Latin document), titled in English, *Constitution on the Sacred Liturgy.* The Council had specifically required a revision of the ordination rites, which Paul VI accomplished in June 1968 (*Constitution on the Sacred Liturgy*, no. 76). As implementation of the reforms continued, he harkened back to Pius XII, who in a 1947 apostolic constitution had spelled out the matter and form for ordination to the diaconate (deacons) and to the presbyterate (priests):

The sole *matter* of the sacred orders of diaconate and presbyterate is the laying on of hands; likewise, the sole *form* is the words determining the application of this matter, which univocally signify the sacramental effects—namely, the power of orders and the grace of the Holy Spirit. (*The Sacrament of Orders*, AAS, 40, 6)

The silent laying on of hands by the bishop and the words of consecration: these are the essence of the priesthood ordination rite and remain as touchstones throughout the ordained priestly ministry. The bishop consecrates priests through an unbroken apostolic succession back to Jesus and the twelve Apostles. The fullness of the priesthood of Jesus Christ rests with the bishop. This laying on of hands in silence signifies the sacramental handing on (*traditio*, in Latin) of the power "to make sacred."

*The silent laying on of hands by the bishop and the words of consecration: these are the essence of the priesthood ordination rite.*

After the ordaining bishop, in silence, lays his hands on the kneeling candidate's head, all the priests who are present follow suit. As the recipient of such a powerful action, I can testify that I did not know specifically (after the bishop, of course) who was laying hands on my head. Yet, the gesture by each member of the body of ordained priests spoke powerfully through the silence of the action. Words fail to explain the powerful effect.

The words of consecration over the ordained priest eloquently express the divine roots of priestly ministry:

Almighty Father, grant to this servant of yours the dignity of the priesthood. Renew within him the Spirit of holiness. As a co-worker with the order of bishops may he be faithful to the ministry that he receives from you, Lord God, and be to others a model of right conduct. (*Rite of Ordination of a Priest*, no. 22)

Dignity. Holiness. Fidelity to the ministry. Model of right conduct. These qualities define the priest in his essence and constitute a mission statement for the ordained minister.

## *Dignity. Holiness. Fidelity to the ministry. Model of right conduct.*

Grant. Renew. These actions speak of the amazing grace and power of God that personally strengthen the ordained priest to live the mission statement. With the help of God, these words of consecration truly matter.

## Litany

Lying face down on a cold marble floor is one of the most humbling experiences imaginable. During the ordination rite, prior to the Litany of Saints, the priesthood candidates, vested in alb and deacon's stole, lie prostrate while the rest of the congregation kneels. The names of saints and holy ones lingered over me; the echoing music and lives hovered over me as I remained face down in this vulnerable position. Mary, Joseph, John the Baptist, Peter and Paul, Andrew, Mary Magdalene, Francis and Dominic, Teresa, Elizabeth Ann Seton, John Neumann, Frances Cabrini, Katherine Drexel—the list seemed never-ending. Throughout this litany I joined in the prayer, speechless while eternity unfolded in this powerful moment of faith.

My personal litany embraced mother, father, godmother, godfather, grandparents, brothers, sisters, aunts, uncles, cousins, teachers, and kind neighbors. For me the list also included priests whom I have been privileged to know in my adult life. I know dozens of priests personally and have met or heard about countless others. The fact that only a handful of them served as models and mentors for me does not speak ill of the others; the example of a few has made a deep impression within my heart.

At the end of the deacon and priesthood rites and before the liturgy of the Eucharist, a priest helps the candidates put on the vestments of the sacrament they have just received: either the deacon's stole and dalmatic (outer vestment) or the priest's stole and chasuble. This assisting priest is usually a mentor or a friend who has been supportive in the candidate's journey to ordination.

*My personal litany embraced mother, father, godmother, godfather, grandparents, brothers, sisters, aunts, uncles, cousins, teachers, and kind neighbors.*

The priest who vested me at my priesthood ordination had inspired me years earlier during his first assignment after ordination. He was the first priest I had ever gotten to know as a person. Although he was young and energetic, he had countless heart problems stemming from a childhood illness that led only a few years later to his early death following a heart transplant. He rode a motorcycle, drove fast cars, planted a garden at his first rectory, and touched the lives of others by a priestly life filled with sincerity and genuineness.

## Promises, Promises

At ordination a priest promises *obedience* to the ordaining bishop and his successors. Diocesan priests do not take a vow of *poverty,* as do members of religious communities in the consecrated life. This difference is one of the least-known facts among people who raise questions about the priesthood. Because priesthood candidates make a commitment to *celibacy* at diaconate ordination, they are already living a celibate life by the time priesthood ordination arrives.

*In truth, love is commitment,*
*a fundamental orientation toward God.*

Promises, vows, and commitments are similar in concept; the difference lies in *who* expresses this decision and *to whom* the statement is addressed. Whatever its form, the commitment must always be firmly rooted in love. Love is so misunderstood and so overused as a term that it has become meaningless to many people and confused with everything from lust to nice feelings to raw emotion. In truth, love is commitment, a fundamental orientation toward God, who makes us a new creation in Christ in communion with neighbor and stranger alike. Love goes beyond a satisfying feeling at liturgy or a sense of accomplishment in an act of service.

Paul's famous words about love from the First Letter to the Corinthians are often included in weddings and other religious and secular ceremonies. His purpose is to speak about the nature of a Christian community, a community that can include any group—as few in number as a married couple and as large as a suburban parish led by a pastor and two assistants. Paul's description of love can serve as the agenda for any ordained minister. Words and actions without love cannot be truly effective.

Love is patient; love is kind; love is not envious or boastful or arrogant or rude. It does not insist on its own way; it is not irritable or resentful; it does not rejoice in wrongdoing but rejoices in the truth. It bears all things, believes all things, hopes all things, endures all things. Love never ends. (1 Corinthians 13:4–8)

Love is never soft, spineless, or devoid of courage. The challenge to the ordained priest is to remain true to love in all seasons, including times when tough love is necessary. Because priests enter ordained ministry motivated by a deep desire to help people, sometimes they get caught in the trap of pleasing people. For many of my brother priests, saying the word *no* becomes a problem; the priest either has a hard time saying no to any request or becomes so disenchanted that he says no to every appeal.

*A heart inspired by God's unconditional love serves as the wellspring for the ordained priest's celibate love.*

Yet, the promise the priest makes at ordination functions not as a prison but rather as an empowerment to serve the people of God. A priest can sustain only by love his promise and his commitment to neighbor and stranger when their interests are other than his own. This kind of love is more powerful than the particular love for another person or the sexual love that is expressed within marriage. This love is rooted in the priest's heartfelt understanding of the unconditional love he receives from God, which allows him to have a heart of flesh, not of stone. A heart inspired by God's unconditional love serves as the wellspring for the ordained priest's celibate love.

As a male, I cannot deny my gender. As a priest, I must deal daily with my gender and my sexual identity. A priest elder once confided to a group of young people, who had inquired about how he deals with sexual temptation, that he expects temptation to end "three days after I'm dead!" His wisdom, born from long and faithful service as a priest, rings true in my heart and brings a smile to my face.

My ordained priesthood is not emasculated, as if I could change myself into a gender-neutral person. I am a man, and who I am as a male is intimately connected with my priestly identity. People fool themselves if they imagine that somehow "Father" is above sexual temptation and feelings. As a celibate, the priest is not married and is not involved in sexual relations, but the priest is not a eunuch! My depth of feeling that moves me to love is rooted in all the feelings that make me male.

Feelings—sexual or otherwise—become an issue when a person acts on them in an unhealthy manner. Furthermore, the church's understanding of celibacy is that it is a freedom rather than a burden. By not being deeply invested in one relationship, the priest is free to be available to all God's people.

*I must address, embrace,*
*and transform these sexual feelings*
*into the core of my loving actions.*

High school students are invariably curious about the priest's sexual experiences. "Can you be a priest if you ever had sex?" "Have you ever fallen in love?" "How do you handle all those feelings?" Yes, some priests are not virgins; some have fallen in love before and may do so again. Healthy priests acknowledge their feelings; instead of entertaining them, they allow them to pass. I must address, embrace, and transform these sexual feelings into the core of my loving actions; otherwise, my ministerial love becomes intellectualized and disconnected from my heart and ultimately from my vocation. "Three days after I'm dead," perhaps I will be beyond these feelings, but for today I am a man, a priest, a complex being with God-given feelings and emotions that enrich my ministerial priesthood.

# Life as a Priest

## In the Midst of God's People

The dinner group of seven friends to which I belong serves as manna from heaven for me and keeps me honest and genuine in my priesthood. This group, all embracing middle age, includes two married couples, a divorced woman, a single woman, and little ole me. The other six were born and raised in the same east-side Buffalo neighborhood (named Lovejoy, one of its main streets). Although I didn't grow up there, they welcomed me into their midst as one of their own.

Self-styled as "the Magnificent Seven," we originated a decade ago as a New Year's Eve gathering of folks who hate New Year's Eve and the over-priced craziness it has become. One couple serve as hosts, and the seven of us dine on homemade French onion soup, surf and turf, twice-baked po-tatoes, tossed salad, ricotta cheese pie, deep chocolate fudge, festive Christmas cookies, and more. Then we lounge around, stuffed and sleepy, playing parlor games like Trivial Pursuit or just talking, laughing, and howl-ing as we wait for the Times Square ball to drop, which prompts us to kiss at midnight and go our separate ways into the new year. Truly, that is more than enough fun for me for one night!

The Magnificent Seven gather throughout the year to renew our grace-filled bonds of friendship. We go away one autumn weekend annually to a picturesque place in western New York's ski country, where we play spirited hands of Hearts, catch up on one another's news, cook, laugh, and carry on without fear of offending the neighbors, for there usually are none except wildlife.

I live my priesthood through my relationship with God and with others. The people in my life, like the Magnificent Seven, keep my sacramental ministry (about another magnificent seven: the sacraments) real and true. I hearken back to the bishop's homily at ordination: "This man, your relative and friend, is now to be raised to the order of priests" (*Rite of Ordination of a Priest*, no.14).

## *I live my priesthood through my relationship with God and with others.*

"Your relative and friend"—the priesthood that I live and perform daily does not drop from out of the blue and disconnect me from others; rather, it emerges from the friendships and family relationships that I renew daily. My priesthood cannot be carried out from an ivory tower; I must live it in the midst of the people of God. For this reason, my Magnificent Seven dinner group—as well as countless friendships with all sorts of folks—nourishes my soul and my ministerial priesthood. Although friends and family keep a priest from taking himself too seriously, he must take seriously the sacramental service to Christ in the "magnificent seven" sacraments to which the Lord calls him daily.

The following words from the ordaining bishop's instructions to the priesthood candidate remind everyone present that sacramental ministry is knitted into the fabric of people's lives.

When you baptize, you will bring men and women into the people of God. In the sacrament of penance, you will forgive sins in the name of

Christ and the Church. With holy oil you will relieve and console the sick. You will celebrate the liturgy and offer thanks and praise to God throughout the day, praying not only for the people of God but for the whole world. *Remember that you are chosen from among God's people and appointed to act for them in relation to God. Do your part in the work of Christ the Priest with genuine joy and love, and attend to the concerns of Christ before your own.* (*Rite of Ordination of a Priest*, no. 14, emphasis added)

By word and action, the ordained priest spiritually nourishes the community of faith. In return the community's consolations and challenges nourish the priest as they journey together to God. Ordained ministry cannot be used as an escape from the complexities of human problems. The church building and the altar serve as a sanctuary only if they are a place of Holy Presence where the priest is called to live the Gospel within the mess of the mundane world. This sanctuary transforms the heart of the priest into a sanctuary, a meeting place, a safe haven, and a holy table where God and humanity can sit down and dine together.

*Ordained ministry cannot be used as an escape from the complexities of human problems.*

## Teaching, Sanctifying, and Shepherding

A priest once suggested to me that ordained ministry demands knowledge of the art and skill of juggling. The priest juggles many demands on his time: being present in the rectory, attending to the sick in the hospital, and visiting parishioners in their homes—all performed at what seems like the same time! This feat makes the act of juggling three eggs or oranges appear simple. At any one moment in ministry, other situations are "up in the air" that the priest does not completely have a handle on or control over. He must attend to everything with a gentle confidence lest all the demands on him come crashing to the ground and he with them.

The priest must be multifaceted; he must become a person of prayer, meditation, and contemplation. He must bear the Divine Presence in the world yet not become part of the world. He is called to serve as a living symbol of action, charity, and hope in the face of apathy, despair, and disbelief. He must preach with wise words that cut through the changing tide of conventional wisdom.

*He is called to serve as a living symbol of action, charity, and hope in the face of apathy, despair, and disbelief.*

While the priest leads a flock, others lead him as a member both of a diocese (led by its bishop) and of the holy, catholic, and apostolic church (led by the bishop of Rome, the pope). Contradictions, complexities, distinctions, and differences define the priest's life as he juggles responsibilities, demands, and identities. He is a leader, a follower, a brother, a father, a teacher, a learner, and, ultimately, a disciple of Christ.

The priest serves Christ, the Teacher, High Priest, and Lord, within a threefold ordained ministry of teaching, sanctifying, and shepherding. By its nature priestly ministry has to juggle and prioritize the demands of each aspect. A priest may hold a strong suit as a teacher, preacher, ritual celebrant, listener, counselor, planner, or organizer. He may especially thrive when working with youth or with older parishioners. Yet, to remain true to his calling, he must extend himself beyond his comfort zone to perform this threefold ministry with its diverse demands to teach, to sanctify, and to shepherd.

One priest described the relationship of an ordained priest to his parish community as a "healthy detachment": graceful involvement in the faith life of the community he is called to serve, without being overly entangled with one aspect of ministry at the expense of everything else. To serve Christ within a faith community, the priest must always be aware of his surroundings and circumstances, his abilities and limitations.

To teach, the priest must be always willing to learn. Opportunities occur daily as long as the senses are open to the experience. Those to whom he ministers teach him in turn, although they certainly are not always aware of it. In my own experience, sick, vulnerable, and chronically ill people unknowingly challenge me to see Christ in their infirmity and in my own. I have learned much about life from those who are confined to a hospital bed and perhaps resting at the threshold of eternal life. As I bring Christ to these encounters, I grow to see him within my own weaknesses and can therefore witness to others the healing strength of Christ, who makes us whole.

*Great failures can be transformed into even greater faithfulness.*

Mistakes serve as teachable moments in ministry if the minister is willing to learn from them. As a teacher of high school students, I have learned a great deal from my mistakes, which often flowed from my inability to allow myself to be vulnerable and to learn from my students. Great failures can be transformed into even greater faithfulness.

It is easy for a priest to point a finger at possible culprits in whatever ministerial disaster he finds himself. During the difficult days of my own ordained ministry, my demonizing others as the cause of controversy only tripped me up and kept me in turmoil. Now, as I look back, I recognize my own faults and, more important, have learned from them. In ministry, no one wins at the "blame game."

To sanctify, the priest is called to sanctity beyond external forms of piety. The manner in which I hold my hands together in prayer does not serve to sanctify the world if my heart does not speak the holiness of God. My holiness must be a true part of me in my actions, my words, and my heart. I cannot simply go through the motions of holiness by observing the church's rubrics to the letter of the law. When I put on the plain white alb, followed by the seasonally colored stole and chasuble for Mass, I do not become different from the person I am when I am away from the altar of sacrifice. I am called to sanctify, no matter what I am wearing, where I am living, or to whom I am speaking. Sanctification does not happen only within the confines of a church building while the priest is wearing vestments. The ordained ministry to sanctify, to which I am called, stems from the sacramental life of the church by which the minister can thrive and grow in holiness.

> *The manner in which I hold my hands together in prayer does not serve to sanctify the world if my heart does not speak the holiness of God.*

My leadership as a priest must ultimately serve the sovereignty of Christ the Lord, who reigns from the throne of the cross. Ordained ministry is leadership in service to Christ, the Good Shepherd, not in service to self. The image of the "servant leader" most clearly conveys the nature of the leadership I am called to exercise within the church.

Leadership is an art and a skill that extend beyond simply telling others what they are supposed to be doing and how I (as leader) am supposed to be in charge of them. The leader stands out in front, in the lead, inspiring those who follow to forge ahead into the unknown. The ordained priest learns leadership skills, but he acquires the art of servant leadership through the grace of God.

*The ordained priest acquires
the art of servant leadership
through the grace of God.*

The leadership modeled by Jesus in his teaching about the good shepherd demands an intimate relationship between leader and followers:

I am the good shepherd. A good shepherd lays down his life for the sheep. The hired hand, who is not the shepherd and does not own the sheep, sees the wolf coming and leaves the sheep and runs away— and the wolf snatches them and scatters them. The hired hand runs away because a hired hand does not care for the sheep. I am the good shepherd. I know my own and my own know me, just as the Father knows me and I know the Father. And I lay down my life for the sheep. (John 10:11–15)

The ordained priesthood that I serve witnesses to the sovereignty of Christ in the servant leadership that I exercise. The faith proclamation that Christ is Lord is more than just a sentence in the creed at Sunday Mass. I hope that my servant leadership inspires deeper belief in Christ and leads to greater charity and hope within people of faith. This leadership of a faith community must be consistent with the life that I lead as a follower of Christ.

## "I Didn't Know You Could Dance!"

I love to dance: fast dance, slow dance, chicken dance, hokey-pokey dance. My dancing days date back to childhood, when my parents insisted that I take a ballroom dancing class offered at public elementary school. I learned the social etiquette that surrounds formal dancing, plus steps to the fox trot, the waltz, and such. Perhaps during the sixties, ballroom dancing appeared to be out of step with the changing times, but it planted within me a love for dancing. From an early age, I learned that dancing is a proper way for a gentleman to socialize with others and make people feel at ease. Manners and etiquette should focus on expressing hospitality toward others and not on making one person feel superior to another.

> *I believe healthy relationships with males and females of different ages strengthen rather than diminish my priesthood.*

Some may suggest that a priest, or a Christian for that matter, should not dance, at least not in public. I am not sure what the rationale is for such a prohibition. Being seen dancing with my arm around a woman could suggest some "special" friendship. I chuckle when I remember how a newly ordained priest (a few years behind me in the seminary) was chastised for dancing with his sister at the reception following his first Mass! I believe healthy relationships with males and females of different ages strengthen rather than diminish my priesthood.

Fr. Walt Szczesny, another priest from Buffalo, adds his thoughts:

I think there are many misconceptions about priesthood. First of all, I remind people that we can still be in love—not sexually, of course— but in meaningful and very fulfilling love relationships with family, friends, and parishioners. That's what really keeps me going. Sometimes, people can fail to see the humanness of priests, for instance:

I can and do enjoy a glass of beer now and then; I like to go to a (Buffalo) Bills game when I get the chance; I run 5K races, and so on.

Preconceived notions of a priest's expected actions and mannerisms are the source of misconceptions that stem from a prior time when the intention of seminary formation was to fit the newly ordained into the priestly "mold." Those new priests, usually products of Catholic schools with six to eight years of seminary training (including collegiate seminary), were approximately twenty-five years of age. In the last two decades, this pattern has become more and more infrequent. Priests are being ordained at an older age and with a variety of life experiences, including public education, secular jobs, and, in rare instances, marriage and parenting.

My first exposure to this phenomenon of "older" priests was at the seminary. The range in age of seminarians at the time (the early 1980s) extended from twenty-one to fifty-five years. "Second-career vocations" began to increase with the realization that age, wisdom, and experience can all serve to form a priest's calling from God. (The term *delayed vocation* mistakenly implies a candidate's reluctance that results in a "delay." Were Simon Peter and the Twelve "at the right age"?) My fellow students at the seminary had pursued occupations ranging from pharmacist, teacher, and social worker to commercial sales and marketing. Each seminarian's arrival at the major seminary with a vast array of experiences enhanced the learning environment for all of us.

## *We learned theology through the lens of life.*

We learned theology through the lens of life that each of us had constructed from his own experience. The diversity of the group in age, intellect, and previous occupation enhanced our learning together in priestly formation. The church and the ordained ministry are all the richer and stronger because of this variety. Unity and uniformity are not synonymous.

Ordained priests can cook, clean, tap dance, write poetry, perform magic tricks, coach football, balance a checkbook, play card games like Hearts and Euchre, tell jokes, plant roses and marigolds, play hockey, sing in a philharmonic choir, teach aerobics, and even wash windows. Priests are not dull men dressed in black but people with diverse experiences and interests. Thank heaven we are not just clones of one another. From the beginnings of the church, as witnessed by the lives of the Apostles, the wide range of humanity has served as the garden in which God cultivates the call to ordained ministry.

*Priests are not dull men dressed in black but people with diverse experiences and interests.*

## Typically Atypical

What makes a rewarding day of ministry? Going to bed tired while knowing that today I may have made a difference in one person's day. I may have three feet of paperwork on my desk, but knowing that I dropped everything for someone in need is a big reward.

Fr. Jim Vacco describes the rewards of ministry this way:

When I hear and see miracles: people are comforted; hope is restored; those who are crying are able to laugh; the people hungry for food or attention receive recognition and dignity; the light shines in those who have been engulfed in the darkness of ignorance or confusion; those who entertained doubt in God find the reality of God through their doubt. I guess, to sum it up, I am rewarded when people are able to smile and "know whom to thank"—not me, but God.

There is probably no such thing as a typical day for a priest. There is probably no such thing as a typical priest! Granted, priests may all look alike in that black suit or in those colorful vestments at the altar during Mass, but they do not stand as carbon copies of one another. Variations extend beyond the obvious one of small, medium, large, and extra large. Priests not only come in different shapes and sizes but also carry out a wide range of responsibilities. They have personal interests that range from country to opera music, from classic literature to contemporary fiction, and from mountain climbing to nap taking.

Most priests work in a parish setting as either the pastor or the parochial vicar (assistant). Some serve within specialized ministries such as education (secondary and college, especially), health care, and prisons. A few hold administrative jobs in Catholic institutions. Typical days for these priests differ greatly from those who work in the usual parish setting.

But what is *typical?* Even within parishes in a specific diocese, the litany of activities varies from urban to suburban to rural faith communities. Parishes are not carbon copies of one another. Every faith community is unique and has a story all its own. The architecture of each church building proclaims the uniqueness of the church community. The mix of people found in a given parish can differ dramatically from that in a neighboring one. The typical eludes an easy, "no muss–no fuss" description.

*What makes a rewarding day of ministry? Going to bed tired while knowing that today I may have made a difference in one person's day.*

# No two days are
## exactly alike.

The term *atypical* might correctly describe the typical day of any priest. No two days are exactly alike. No matter how well I schedule and organize my day planner, the layout does not always match the output when the day is done. The common variable that marks the atypical day is *people*. As I sit in the rectory office going through the day's mail or planning my schedule of hospital calls and nursing home visits, I cannot predict the needs of the stranger who will ring the rectory doorbell or anonymously reach out over the telephone. As I prepare for tonight's meeting of the liturgy committee to plan Holy Week services, a funeral call may come in that turns the typical upside down for the next three days. Perhaps a stalwart of that liturgy committee dies unexpectedly at an early age. Life stops, or at least the planned part of a priest's life pauses as I respond to the family numbed by loss.

Still, some priestly activities are performed daily, no matter the parish, diocese, or specific ordained ministry. Even those in specialized ministries, such as teaching, often start the day with an early morning Mass. Some parishes have multiple daily Masses, often matching the number of priests who live in the rectory. Whether he is presiding or concelebrating, the priest celebrates and receives the Eucharist daily.

For example, ever since 1993, when I started teaching high school, I have presided at an early (6:30 or 6:45 a.m.) eucharistic celebration. Members of a steady and faithful congregation (around ten!) emerge from their homes into the dawn's early light of each new day. On arriving, they scatter throughout the body of the church. (Some parishes are fortunate enough to have a small daily Mass chapel that provides a more intimate setting.) Working people and retired folks join quietly and simply to offer praise, thanks, and the day to God.

Solemnities, feast days, fast days, seasons, and normal weekdays mark the rhythm of this daily ritual. Every two years, the congregation proceeds anew through the list of weekday and seasonal readings that cover the bulk of the Old and the New Testament. Usually, I share a one-to two-minute homiletic reflection with the congregation, always cognizant of the tight time frame for many in attendance. Sometimes people rush off to work with the final blessing echoing in their ears and holy water dripping from their hands.

Parish priests often will deal with funerals on weekday mornings, providing a ministry of bereavement and presence in the context of the eucharistic celebration. Usually, only family members and close friends attend these funerals, and rarely is the church packed with mourners. Funeral ministry can deeply touch the lives of those who are open to the Gospel message, including mourners who are not members of a church and those who are alienated from the Catholic church.

## *Faith community develops through dialogue and conversation.*

Ministry of presence often occupies the remainder of the priest's day—presence to schoolchildren and teachers in an adjoining parish elementary school, to the elderly people of the parish, to people in need of spiritual direction, and to others. As the priest gets to know people, whatever their age, they will get to know him as well. A faith community develops through dialogue and conversation. One-to-one encounters, whatever the situation, are an integral part of daily ministry for the ordained priest. He carries this ministry of presence to hospitals and nursing homes, not only to patients but also to caregivers. Anointing of the sick brings the Crucified and Risen Christ's healing presence to the suffering endured by all.

Meetings, meetings, and more meetings mark the evenings. Endless meetings—these are important gatherings nonetheless. Focused and productive meetings of parish pastoral councils, liturgy committees, finance boards, and other groups allow faith community members to take ownership of the spiritual growth of their community. The priest's or parish staff's leadership and guidance of these subcommunities within the greater faith community empower everyone involved.

A typical problem for most priests is that of time, especially the lack of it. How does "Father" find enough time to keep himself spiritually, mentally, physically, and emotionally healthy? Even planning a religious regimen of prayer, spiritual reading, exercise, and social time with priest and lay friends does not guarantee that any of it will happen.

An older priest once advised me that the workday is divided into three parts and that one part (morning, afternoon, or evening) needs to be reserved for a priest's personal activities. As it is, the typical ministry day can extend to between ten and twelve hours. Without personal time the priest finds burnout lurking in the shadows and waiting to pounce on the exhausted minister. Another priest once counseled a group of us to consider a day off each week (usually other than Sunday) to be as sacred as the Sabbath. A seminary professor once jokingly advised, "Once a day out of the rectory, once a week out of town, once a month out of state, and once a year out of the country."

*An older priest once advised me that the workday is divided into three parts and that one part needs to be reserved for a priest's personal activities.*

Sunday is a bit more typical than weekdays. Everybody goes to church on Sunday or at least is supposed to! Sunday morning, as well as Saturday evening, is spent in church presiding at the Eucharist, helping to distribute Communion, greeting people at the door, having a few minutes of conversation with liturgical ministers, and briefly seeing a great number of the faith community. Concentrated activity and participation by lots of people demand an invigorating ministry of presence throughout the weekend.

The effort is not as much physical as emotional and mental. Presiding, preaching, and being ministerially present at multiple eucharistic celebrations are far more draining than people imagine. Some priests take the opportunity to relax on Sunday afternoon or evening, although certain parishes have regular Sunday evening activities, such as youth groups and religious education.

In addition, weekends are typically marked by Saturday weddings and an occasional funeral, by Sunday afternoon baptisms, and at times by special events at the cathedral. These are in addition to the unexpected as well as to the full plate of Sunday morning offerings. Honest, earnest, and final homily preparation takes place Saturday morning, if something else isn't already scheduled. The lay pastoral staff do not always work in the office on weekends, but the phone still rings—endlessly.

Responsibility rests with the priest to strike a balance so that the fifth phone call on Saturday asking for the Sunday Mass schedule does not result in Father's giving an inappropriate or rude response to the inquirer. Prayer time, personal time, and social time make ministry time more meaningful.

## Behind Rectory Doors

As a child I remember the bright red brick rectory that silently stood next to the bigger-than-life red brick downtown church from which people streamed to their cars parked nearby. The priest's house sparked the imagination of this child—those large windows and that forbidding oak front door! Several priests used to live in that enormous home, which few in the parish ever saw, save for the formal front vestibule. Often the live-in housekeeper served as the gatekeeper. The housekeeper ruled the rectory (her home as well) with a rolling pin firmly in hand. Those were the days before a pastoral staff that now includes secretaries and bookkeepers.

By the time I was ordained in the mid-1980s, this scene (for the most part) had begun to change for a variety of reasons. For one thing, with the decreasing number of clergy, the days of the full-to-the-brim rectory were dwindling. The well-appointed parish house remained forbidding in outer appearance but became quite empty of residents.

However, as participation in parish life started to open up, so did the rectory. The vast spaces began to be used frequently for meetings of parish organizations and committees. Parishioners made themselves at home in this rather large house with multiple suites of sitting rooms, bedrooms, and bathrooms designed for three, four, or five resident priests.

With the advent of parish life and activities within the walls of the rectory, a conflict began to develop as to its purpose. Is the building a home, an office, both, or neither? With fewer priests living there, could the former model of "community" life for secular priests endure? In one rectory, my suite (bedroom, bathroom, and sitting room) was on the first floor. This busy suburban parish had activities and meetings on nearly a nightly basis. I used to change into my plaid nightshirt and gray sweats right after dinner, to be comfortable while preparing for the next day in the classroom. Walking into the hallway outside my rooms was always at my own risk, for I never knew whom I would be meeting across the hall in the formal dining room or living room. Carefully timed dashes to the kitchen for a snack were required lest I be caught in my slumberwear!

*With the advent of parish life and activities within the walls of the rectory, a conflict began to develop as to its purpose.*

If the opportunity arose, some parishes moved their offices and meeting rooms elsewhere or found modest, homelike accommodations for the priest resident(s). But the rectory remains the norm for the ordained priest.

I will be honest. I have never cared much for rectories. It is not a question of their opulence, because not all rectories are large or have decent and comfortable furniture; in fact, I have visited a couple of rectories I might describe as tattered. Many rectories do not have a homey feel to them for one main reason: living in the same place where you work and with the same people you work with (even though they are brother priests) creates a challenge to that homey feel. No escape from "the firm" seems possible, and it is hard to feel at home when everything you are sitting on is borrowed for the time you are assigned to the parish.

My best living situation was during the five years I lived in a quaint house, separate from the office, while working in college campus ministry at the Fredonia Newman Center. The small, rustic, two-bedroom house seemed more like a home than an institution.

*Communication across the generations and through the uniqueness of each priest must mark rectory life, personally and professionally.*

Yet, the rectory is in the cards that most priests are dealt, and living as a diocesan priest with other priests "in community" remains a possibility. Communication across the generations and through the uniqueness of each priest must mark rectory life, personally and professionally. Whose house is it, anyway? is the question that priest residents must answer constantly in relationship to their parish faith community. All parties involved, including the parish members, must not ignore how that parish house is made into a home for the ordained ministers. Perhaps priests can find another way to live in relationship to their parish faith communities. Looking beyond the rectory model may allow a new vision to emerge.

I have lived in a number of rectories and with several priests. My brother priests have been silent, talkative, amusing, serious, arrogant, humble, hostile, meek, morose, and mean. I am sure I am not the easiest person to live with either, although I generally enjoy my own company! However, the rectory never seems to afford the opportunity for priests truly to live together. It is so easy for priests to go into their own room after supper, turn on their own television, and watch situation comedies in solitary confinement.

Even if a priest is living by himself in a rectory, it is too easy to migrate down the hall or downstairs to his desk, where the paperwork never goes away. The priest must develop a sense of sanctuary and safe haven within hearth and home where he can personally recharge his batteries off duty without always having to face work.

*The priest must develop a sense of sanctuary . . . where he can personally recharge his batteries.*

Seminary training does not fully prepare the young cleric for the rectory phenomenon. Living and working in the same place without strongly developed communication skills and a secure sense of self can lead to personal and ministerial unhappiness down the road. So often in the past, young priests found ministry a challenge because of the difficulties of rectory life, where there never seemed to be anywhere to escape when problems arose with coworkers or brother priests.

Even if a priest lives separately from the workplace, the need remains for communication skills among coworkers—ordained and nonordained.

Wherever the priest lives and whatever he does in ministry are always in relationship to others, whether they are parishioners, brother priests, or God.

The ordained ministerial life is not a perfect life. Pressures and expectations hurtle at you from all directions, and it is easy to cast stones at the church's flaws. In the long run, these stones only break things, not mend them. As is the case with any state in life—married or single, brother or sister, ordained or nonordained—how you handle the less-than-perfect situation is the point where your faith life unfolds.

> *The ordained ministerial life*
> *is not a perfect life.*

Rectory life may not be the ideal situation for ordained ministers, but they embrace the life of grace within their call to ministry even in the less-than-ideal situations. Christ's presence seeks a dwelling place within the imperfect to transform it through divine grace.

# Conclusion

## Fostering Vocations

Whose job is it, anyway, to develop vocations to the priesthood in the future? Is it the vocation directors of the dioceses and the religious orders? the bishops? the priests? the parents? the teachers? We pray for vocations and celebrate special Sundays to promote vocations. The need for ordained priests becomes more apparent daily. Believers continue to take responsibility for their spiritual life. Yet, I am not sure that people in the pews recognize the vocation responsibility to be their own. These words from the *Code of Canon Law* serve to frame the responsibility globally:

> A duty rests upon the entire Christian community to foster vocations so that sufficient provision is made for the needs of the sacred ministry throughout the entire Church; Christian families, educators, and in a special way priests, especially pastors, are particularly bound by this duty. Since it is principally the concern of diocesan bishops to promote vocations, they should instruct the people entrusted to them concerning the importance of the sacred ministry and the necessity of ministers in the

church; therefore, they are to encourage and support endeavors to foster vocations by means of projects especially established for that purpose. (Canon 233)

Teachers and religious catechists play a formative role in the developmental process of the young. The virtue of selfless service to others is witnessed by their example in the classroom.

Family time spent together at the table, in conversation, at church, and even in community-service activities can fan the flames of a priestly vocation. We should not shortchange the power of family and the role of parents as primary educators of their children. Parents desire the best for their children but often keep them so busy that they miss opportunities at hand within the family itself.

Promotion of vocations should flow naturally through priests who are happy and healthy in their ministry. The call to ordained priesthood comes through the sound of many voices, in fact, the voices of the entire Christian community. Family life and school life cultivate the call. Leaders in faith communities, from pastors to presidents of parish organizations, speak the call through articulation of awareness. That awareness is spoken in the clear voicing of the need for leadership, as well as through the modeling of servant leadership. A vocation emerges from within, but it is cultivated from the outside. The seminary is important in caring for the seed of the vocation, but planting that seed and aiding in the harvest are the proper work of the whole body of believers. The entire community of faith, the church, is called in Baptism to cultivate vocations.

It is my sincere hope that these words will stimulate your call and duty to foster vocations—including the one that might be in your heart. The vocation responsibility rests with the entire people of God because it is through their voices that the Divine Voice is heard.

# For Further Reading

"Life as a Vocation: Message of the Holy Father for the 38th World Day of Prayer for Vocations," 6 May 2001, by Pope John Paul II, Vatican City Web site, http://www.vatican.va/holy_father/john_paul_ii/ messages/vocations/documents/hf_jp-ii_mes_20001125_xxxviii- voc-2001_en.html. Accessed 5 July 2001.

National Coalition for Church Vocations (Chicago, IL), Web site, http://www.nccv-vocations.org. Accessed 5 July 2001.

"The Priest and the Third Christian Millennium: Teacher of the Word, Minister of the Sacraments, and Leader of the Community," by the Congregation for the Clergy, 19 March 1999 (Vatican City, 1999), www.vocations.com/priest/ priest3m.html. Accessed 5 July 2001.

*Priesthood in the Modern World*, edited by Karen Sue Smith (New York: Sheed and Ward, 1999).

*A Spiritual Theology of the Priesthood: The Mystery of Christ and the Mission of the Priest*, by Dermot Power (Washington: Catholic University of America Press, 1998).

*The Spirituality of the Diocesan Priest*, edited by Donald Cozzens (Collegeville, MN: Liturgical Press, 1997).

*The Theology of Priesthood*, edited by Donald J. Goergen and Ann Garrido (Collegeville, MN: Liturgical Press, 2000).

Vocations Online, Web site sponsored by the Diocese of Joliet Vocations Office (Joliet, IL), http://www.vocations.com. Accessed 5 July 2001.

# Acknowledgments *(continued from page 4)*

The Scripture quotations contained herein are from the New Revised Standard Version of the Bible Catholic Edition. Copyright © 1993 and 1989 by the Division of Christian Education of the National Council of the Churches of Christ in the United States of America. Used by permission. All rights reserved.

The quote on pages 9–10 and 13 is from *Evangelium Vitae,* by Pope John Paul II (Washington, DC: United States Catholic Conference, 1995), number 61. Copyright © 1995 by the United States Catholic Conference. All rights reserved.

The quotes on pages 23, 24, 37–38, 44, and 44–45 are from *Rite of Ordination of a Priest,* in *The Rites of the Catholic Church: Study Edition*, vol. 2. Prepared by the International Commission on English in the Liturgy (Collegeville, MN: Liturgical Press, 1991), numbers 25, 13, 22, and 14 (twice), respectively. Copyright © 1980 by Pueblo Publishing Company. Copyright © 1991 by the Order of St. Benedict, Collegeville, MN. All rights reserved.

The material on page 29 and the quotes on pages 31, 31–32, and 62 are from the *Code of Canon Law: Latin-English Edition*, translation prepared under the auspices of the Canon Law Society of America (Washington, DC: Canon Law Society of America, 1983), numbers 1032, 1031, 232, 235, 241, 244, 245, and 233, respectively. Copyright © 1983 by the Canon Law Society of America. All rights reserved.

The quotes on pages 33 and 34 are from *The Institution of Readers and Acolytes,* in *The Rites of the Catholic Church: Study Edition*, vol. 2. Prepared by the International Commission on English in the Liturgy (Collegeville, MN: Liturgical Press, 1991), numbers 4, 7, and 4, respectively. Copyright © 1980 by Pueblo Publishing Company. Copyright © 1991 by the Order of St. Benedict, Collegeville, MN. The English translation of *The Institution of Readers and Acolytes* is by the International Committee on English in the Liturgy. Copyright © 1976 by the International Committee on English in the Liturgy. All rights reserved.

The material on page 36 refers to the *Constitution on the Sacred Liturgy*, by the Second Vatican Council, 4 December 1963 (Collegeville, MN: Liturgical Press, 1963), number 76.

The quote on page 37 is from *The Sacrament of Orders (Sacramentum Ordinis)*, Apostolic Constitution by Pope Pius XII, 30 November 1947, in *Acta Apostolicae Sedis*, 1948, vol. 40, page 6, cited in *Approval of the New Rites for the Ordination of Deacons, Presbyters, and Bishops*, Apostolic Constitution by Pope Paul VI, 18 June 1968, in *The Rites of the Catholic Church as Revised by the Second Vatican Council* (New York: Pueblo Publishing, 1980), page 46.